BASIC BIOGRAPHIES

Thomas Edison

by Susan Kesselring

Thomas Edison had lots of good ideas. He used his ideas to **invent** new things.

Thomas Edison invented new things in his workshop.

Thomas was born in Ohio on February 11, 1847. When he was young, he was sick a lot. But he was always asking his parents how things worked.

Thomas (right) visits his childhood home.

School was hard for Thomas. So his mother taught him at home instead. He liked that much better.

Thomas was four years old in this photograph.

Thomas could not hear very well. But that never held him back. He liked to try out his big ideas.

Thomas had many ideas when he was young.

9

Thomas had a job when he was only 13. He learned how to use a **telegraph**. He started to make **inventions**. One of his first inventions was a new voting **machine**.

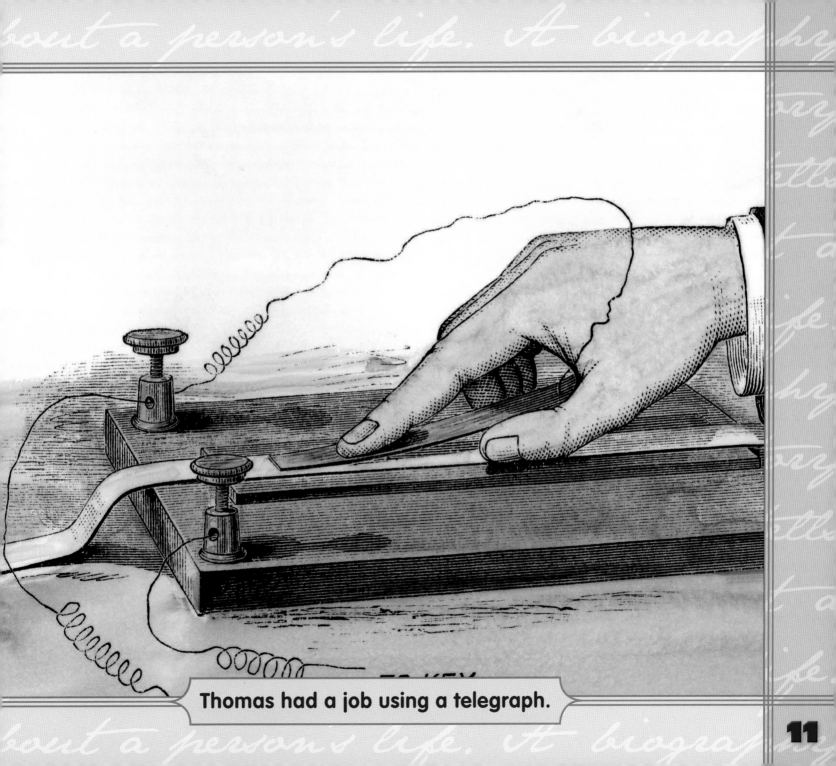

Thomas had a job using a telegraph.

Thomas worked hard on his ideas. Soon he made a machine that helped the telegraph work better than it did before. Then he made the first **phonograph**.

The phonograph could record and play back sounds.

Some people think Thomas Edison invented the light bulb. He did not. He made a light bulb that worked better than earlier models.

Thomas did not invent the light bulb.

Thomas started a workshop.
Many other people helped
him invent wonderful things.

Thomas worked with other inventors.

Later, Thomas found a way to get power for heat and light into homes. He also made the first machine that could show movies.

Thomas's machines put power in people's homes.

Thomas invented more than 1,000 things. He died in 1931. His work made life better for many people.

Thomas was a great inventor.

Glossary

invent (in-VENT): To invent is to come up with an idea and make something new. Someone invented the light bulb.

invention (in-VEN-shun): An invention is something that no one has made before. Some inventions make life better.

machine (muh-SHEEN): A machine is a thing with different parts that work together to do a job. Many machines make work easier.

phonograph (FOH-nuh-graf): A phonograph is a machine that can record and play sounds. People used phonographs to listen to music.

telegraph (TEL-uh-graf): A telegraph is a machine that sends messages in code. Thomas made a better kind of telegraph.

To Find Out More

Books

deMauro, Lisa, et al. *Thomas Edison: A Brilliant Inventor.* New York: HarperCollins Publishers, 2005.

Goldsmith, Howard. *Thomas Edison to the Rescue.* New York: Simon & Schuster, 2003.

MacLeod, Elizabeth. *Thomas Edison.* Toronto, Ontario: Kids Can Press, Inc., 2008.

Web Sites

Visit our Web site for links about Thomas Edison: *childsworld.com/links*

Note to Parents, Teachers, and Librarians: We routinely verify our Web links to make sure they are safe and active sites. So encourage your readers to check them out!

Index

About the Author

Susan Kesselring has taught all ages of children from preschool through grade 8. She has been a certified Reading Recovery teacher and director of a preschool. She loves to help children get excited about learning. Family, friends, books, music, and her dog, Lois Lane, are some of her favorite things.

On the cover: Thomas Edison stands in his laboratory in 1911.

Published by The Child's World®
1980 Lookout Drive • Mankato, MN 56003-1705
800-599-READ • www.childsworld.com

ACKNOWLEDGMENTS
The Child's World®: Mary Berendes, Publishing Director
The Design Lab: Design and production
Red Line Editorial: Editorial direction

PHOTO CREDITS: Library of Congress, cover, 13, 21; Yegor Korzh/iStockphoto, cover, 1, 14; The Print Collector/Photolibrary, 3; AP Images, 5, 15, 17; U.S. Department of the Interior, National Park Service, Thomas Edison National Historical Park, 7, 9; North Wind Picture Archives/Photolibrary, 11, 19

Printed in the United States of America in Mankato, Minnesota.
November 2009
F11460

LIBRARY OF CONGRESS CATALOGING-IN-PUBLICATION DATA
Kesselring, Susan.
  Thomas Edison / by Susan Kesselring.
    p. cm. — (Basic biographies)
  Includes index.
  ISBN 978-1-60253-345-5 (lib. bd. : alk. paper)
  1. Edison, Thomas A. (Thomas Alva), 1847–1931—Juvenile literature.
2. Inventors—United States—Biography—Juvenile literature. 3. Electrical engineers—United States—Biography—Juvenile literature. I. Title. II. Series.
  TK140.E3K47 2010
  621.3092—dc22 [B]   2009029374